A Great Day for a Ride

Written by Diana Noonan
Illustrated by Anna-Maria Crum

Characters

Queen

Royal Advisor 2

Royal Advisor 1

Royal Advisor 3

Royal Advisor 4

Royal Advisors 1, 2, 3, and 4: Good morning, Your Majesty.

Queen: Yes, indeed, Royal **Advisors**, it's a very good morning – a great way to start the new century. It's hard to believe it's 1800 already! It seems like just yesterday that we were in the 1700s.

Royal Advisor 1: That's very **perceptive** of you – a new century *has* dawned, Your Majesty.

Queen: How I wish I could fly. What a great day it would be for flying!

Royal Advisor 3: Yes, Your Majesty. The sun is shining, the birds are singing…

Royal Advisor 1: And the royal lake is as smooth and glimmering as your finest mirror – it's an ideal day to tone your physique by rowing, Your Powerfulness.

Royal Advisor 2: Or flying the royal kite, Ma'am.

Royal Advisor 3: Or taking a stroll in the royal gardens.

Royal Advisor 4 (*to himself*):
Nothing is ever that uncomplicated with this Queen.

Queen: Oh, how very **tedious** that all sounds. Can't you think of something more exciting for me to do?

Royal Advisor 4 (*to himself*):
I thought she was in one of those moods.

Royal Advisor 1: Here's a **scintillating** suggestion – you might enjoy an **equestrian** adventure. Galloping on a fiery **steed** is always exciting, Majesty of Mine.

Royal Advisor 2: Do you mean a little fox hunting?

Royal Advisor 3: Or how about a little **archery**?

Queen: I mean nothing of the sort. Aren't you listening? I said something exciting. E. X. C. I. T. I. N. G – exciting!

Royal Advisor 4 (*to himself*):
All signs point to this being a challenging day in the palace.

Royal Advisor 1: Your Royalness, we seek your wisdom on these matters – what, to you, would signify a **superlative** day?

Queen: What I have in mind is…

Royal Advisors 1, 2, 3, and 4:
Y-e-s?

Queen: A bicycle ride in the country.

Royal Advisor 4 (*to himself*):
I just knew that trouble was **looming**.

Royal Advisor 2: A bicycle ride, Your Majesty?

Royal Advisor 3: In the country, Your Royal Highness?

Queen: That's what I said.

Royal Advisor 3: There's just the teensiest, weensiest little problem, Ma'am.

Queen: What do you mean "problem"? Surely it's your job to overcome problems, especially teensy, weensy problems.

Royal Advisor 1: Who among us shall reveal the regrettable truth?

Royal Advisor 2: Not me.

Royal Advisor 3: Definitely not me.

Royal Advisor 4 (*quietly, to himself*):
As usual, it's left up to me to do the dirty work. **(*louder*)** Well, Your Majesty, I regret to inform you that a bicycle ride in the country is not possible… well, not today, anyway.

Queen: Not possible! Not possible! But of course it's possible. If I want it, then it must be possible. It's your job to make it possible!

Royal Advisor 3: The problem is, Ma'am, that the, um, the bicycle… well, you see, it hasn't been invented yet.

Royal Advisor 1: Of course, this much-desired mode of transportation is fairly **imminent**, Your Royal Impatience.

Royal Advisor 2: Only another 40 years, in fact.

Royal Advisor 1: Thirty-nine, to be precise. It will be in the year 1839 that a creative genius named Kirkpatrick Macmillan will invent the bicycle.

Queen: That sounds like a good Scottish name. Why don't you find him and get him to work on this today? You know, just hurry him along a little.

Royal Advisor 3: I don't think that's possible, Your Majesty. You see, Kirkpatrick Macmillan will be a Scottish **blacksmith** when he invents the bicycle, but he isn't old enough to be a blacksmith now. In fact, he hasn't even been born yet.

Royal Advisor 1: Aha, Your Regal **Orneriness**, might I suggest an alternative? There is a bicycle **prototype**, much like a scooter, but you sit upon it and use your feet to propel it along the ground.

Royal Advisor 2: If you can wait 39 years, Kirkpatrick Macmillan will invent some little things called pedals to make riding easier…

Royal Advisor 4: …and faster.

Queen: Fine. I'm ready to try out whatever you can come up with.

Royal Advisor 2: The best we can do for you right now is the "dandy horse". It's more of a *walking* **contraption** than a bicycle.

Royal Advisor 3: I must warn Your Majesty that the dandy horse is quite slow, and it's not easy to ride.

Queen: I don't like the sound of that at all.

Royal Advisor 2: I believe that they can be quite enjoyable, Your Majesty, but they're not the sort of thing you would ride through the countryside.

Royal Advisor 4: You see, it was invented in France…

Royal Advisor 3: …just ten years ago, in 1790. The king uses it to push himself around the royal gardens.

Queen: I'd rather wait for the blacksmith from Scotland with his… what are they called?

Royal Advisor 2: Pedals, Your Highness.

Royal Advisor 3: Macmillan will base his bicycle design with pedals on the dandy horse.

Royal Advisor 1: A rider on his bicycle will sit on a seat between the two wheels.

Queen: That sounds fine – why don't you fools put that together this morning, and then I'll take it out this afternoon?

Royal Advisor 2: Well... you see, even with all the blacksmith's skill with metals, this will be a large, heavy contraption.

Royal Advisor 3: It will weigh as much as a ten-year-old child. One will need considerable strength and stamina to ride it.

Royal Advisor 4: This won't be a problem for a fit young blacksmith such as Macmillan, but it wouldn't be as easy for one such as Your Royal Highness!

Royal Advisor 1: The scenario worsens – there is a comfort issue. I have it on reliable authority that the wheels of the first bicycle will be constructed from wood, with iron tyres.

Queen: I do declare, that sounds like a very bumpy ride and not at all comfortable on my royal...

Royal Advisor 2: ...in another 80 years, your ride would be more comfortable, Ma'am.

Royal Advisor 1: **Indubitably** – in 1880, another Scottish gentleman, by the name of Dunlop, will invent rubber tyres filled with air – tyres designed to cushion you over those **repellent** potholes, Your Delicate-ness.

Royal Advisor 3: If only we could wait around for another 170 years – then we'd have bicycles with gears!

Queen: Well, I'm not waiting around any longer. If you can't find something **exhilarating** for me to do, I shall just watch television all day.

Royal Advisor 1: Did she say what I thought she said?

Royal Advisor 2: I'm afraid she did.

Royal Advisor 3: Who's going to tell her that television hasn't been invented yet?

Royal Advisor 4: Why are you all looking at me like that? Why do I always have to tell the Queen that she can't do what she wants to do?

Queen: Come along, who's got the remote?

Royal Advisor 4: Um, Your Majesty, I have some rather upsetting news for you, and you won't be hearing about it on the television…